Sai Vani

Inspiring Words of Sai Baba

With

Aushim Khetarpal

Copyright © 2024 Aushim Khetarpal

This is a work of nonfiction. The events and the incidents mentioned in the book are true and real. However, some names and characteristics have been changed, some events have been compressed, and some dialogues have been recreated.

All Rights Reserved

First Edition: December 2024

Printed in India

ISBN: 978-81-981861-9-5

Publisher: Aum Sportainment Pvt. Ltd.
39-A, Ground Floor, DDA Flat,
Shahpur Jat, New Delhi - 110049
E-mail : aum.sportainment@gmail.com

Illustration: Nikshubha Srivastava

No part of this book may be reproduced, or stored in a retrieval system, or transmitted in any form or by any means, electronic, mechanical, photocopying, recording, or otherwise, without express written permission of the publisher.

CONNECT WITH US

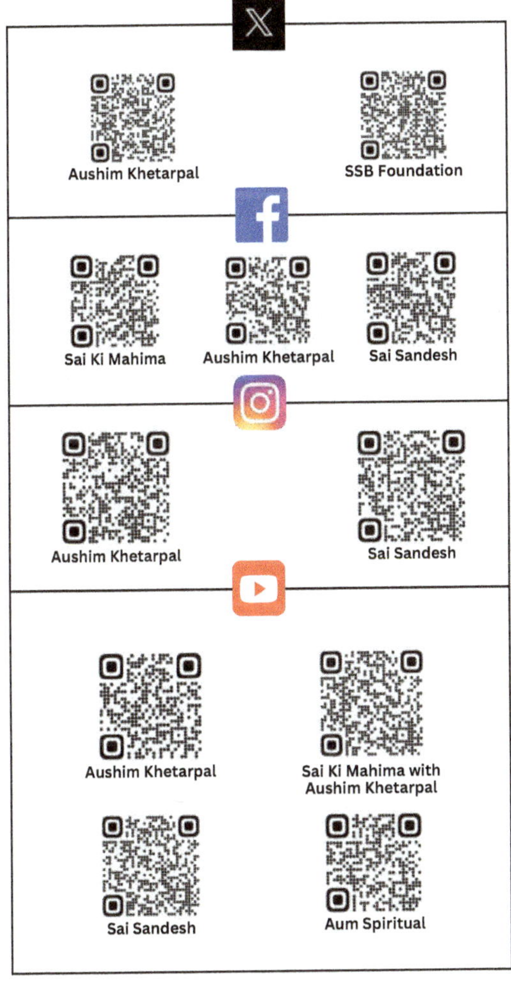

ॐ
साईराम

From the Author's Desk

In this book, we will explore the spiritual significance and the role Sai Baba plays in providing solace and knowledge to individuals. Through the experience of a devotee, we will delve deeply into the power of devotion and its profound impact on the mind. Today, we will learn about the fascinating life of Sai Baba. It is indeed remarkable how a simple sentence can hold so much power and influence.

"Sai Vani" is a conversation between Sai Baba and his devotee. Additionally, this book glorifies the "Sai Baba Satcharitra". Along with this, the conversation explains the saga of Sai Baba and spirituality. The main objective of this work is to bring the image of the Sai Satcharitra and the spiritual brilliance of Baba to the masses. It is hoped that through Baba's life events, parables, and teachings, good resolutions will be awakened in people, and with his grace, they will manifest in their actions. People's thoughts should become positive. Let them walk peacefully on the straight paths of steady temperament and sweet behavior, and lead a stress-free, healthy life. May a sense of community develop within everyone, and may everyone's world be filled with happiness.

One book that is gaining popularity in spreading the messages of positive mornings is "Sai Vani". This book offers a wide range of options for morning messages. It provides readers with an opportunity to start their day positively and experience the transformative power of positive thinking. As you progress through this book, you will discover that it is not just a collection of morning messages, but a journey with Baba as your spiritual guide. This journey is a transformative experience. Each message helps you connect with your inner self and guides you towards a more meaningful and purposeful life.

One remarkable aspect of "Sai Vani" is that it helps you in completing any unfinished tasks. As you delve deeper into the book, you will find that your tasks have been completed with ease. This is because the positive energy generated from the morning messages motivates you to take the necessary actions. In this book, we will explore the spiritual significance and Sai Baba's role in providing comfort and knowledge to individuals. Through the experience of a devotee, we will deeply examine the power of devotion and its impact on the mind. Today, we will learn about the fascinating life of Sai Baba. It is indeed noteworthy how a simple sentence can possess such power and influence.

A major aspect emphasized in the book is the practice of "Jap" (chanting) and "Shanti Charitra" (peaceful character). These practices involve repeating a sacred mantra or chant and developing a peaceful and virtuous character. By incorporating these practices into your morning routine, you can experience a deep sense of inner peace and create a positive atmosphere throughout your day.

The author, controller, and compiler of this book is none other than Sachidanand Sadguru Sai Baba himself. He is the one who inspires and encourages the performers on the stage. He fills the mind with new ideas, empowers experiences, and shapes expressions into tangible forms. Sai Baba's image pulls us to heights that even the sun and the poet cannot reach, initiating a sequence of actions that starts from imagination and leads to real-world deeds.

The birth of a creation!

Aushim Khetarpal

The Power of Positive Morning Messages

Let's start the book by emphasizing on the importance of sending and receiving positive messages in the morning. Starting your day on a positive note can significantly impact your overall well-being. It sets the tone for the rest of the day and can bring about a meaningful shift in your outlook. In this chapter, we will explore the power of positive morning messages and how they can transform your life!

Positive morning messages not only have the ability to uplift the mood of those who hear them but also positively affect the people around them. They generate a sense of positivity and create a ripple of good vibes that lasts throughout the day. When you wake up and read such a message, it can change the course of your entire day, making it more productive and fulfilling.

By committing to incorporating positive morning messages into your daily routine, you open yourself up to a world of endless possibilities. Each message acts as a catalyst, inspiring you to embrace new opportunities and bring positive changes into your life. The life-changing potential lies within these positive messages. Through this simple practice, you will gradually advance toward overall well-being. You will also inevitably witness transformative success in your relationships.

Conclusion

Aushim - Starting your day with positive morning messages can have a profound impact on your life. The book "Sai Vani" offers a treasure trove of uplifting messages that can set the tone for a successful and fulfilling day. By incorporating these messages into your morning routine, you can harness the power of positivity and experience life-changing transformations. So why wait? Begin your journey today towards a brighter and more positive future!

Faith and Belief

Many people in this world believe in Sai Baba, while others
do not. However, there comes a time when everyone begins
to believe in Sai Baba. Why does this happen?

The undeniable answer to this is faith.

The foundation of faith is belief. When belief takes root in the heart, circumstances change, and challenges become surmountable. The world begins to feel transformed as if an entire era has shifted.

Whether the world accepts Sai Baba as God or not, it is an undisputed truth that Sai Baba is a true Guru and a genuine guide. Sai Baba guided his devotees on the right path.

Even after a century of his Mahasamadhi, his teachings and lessons are still capable of guiding the world on the right path.

Devotees have revered Sai Baba as the embodiment of supreme powers like Ram, Krishna, Buddha, Shiva, Nanak, and Jesus. Many of Sai Baba's devotees have directly felt the presence of his divine authority within their hearts.

Sai Baba has bestowed his true devotees with invaluable experiences from time to time. This is Sai Baba's boundless grace upon his true devotee. Even today, millions of people are walking on the righteous path because of Sai Baba's teachings. It is this faith that forms the core foundation of this book.

My First Meeting with Baba

In the depths of the night, while journeying within my mind, I found myself seeking solace beneath a neem tree. Lost in his name, immersed in meditation, I was illuminated by the divine flame of the sage. This was my first encounter with Baba. As I listened to his stories, I sought answers and found refuge in his teachings. And what did Baba give me?

He gave me his name. At that moment, I transcended, and my journey of meditation began.

As part of my inner strength, Baba says to me, "Do not cry anymore, remain under my care. Your pain is mine, and my strength is your strength. Lead, dispel the darkness of confusion, and spread the light."

In these simple words, Baba reveals a profound truth, which I wish to convey to all of you through this book.

The path to peace and strength lies within us. By surrendering to the divine light, we can find solace and strength. Let us explore how we can embrace the divine light and transform our lives. Let us begin this journey by reflecting on our inner selves. Take time each day to sit quietly and observe your thoughts and emotions. This practice of self-reflection will help you gain clarity and reveal your true potential. Release the thoughts that weigh you down. Let go of past grievances, regrets, and negative emotions. Forgiveness and acceptance are powerful tools. They will free your soul and allow the divine flame within you to burn brighter. Appreciate the blessings in your life. Cultivate gratitude for both big and small things. Gratitude opens your heart and connects you to the divine energy that surrounds us all. Nourish your soul with positive experiences. Engage in activities that bring you joy, peace, and satisfaction, whether it's spending time in nature, pursuing a hobby, or connecting with loved ones. Always prioritize self-care

and soul nourishment. Along with this, practice love and compassion for yourself and others.

Nourish your soul with positive experiences. Engage in activities that bring you joy, peace, and fulfillment. Whether it's spending time in nature, pursuing a hobby, or connecting with loved ones, always prioritize self-care and soul nourishment. Along with this, practice love and compassion for yourself and others.

By doing so, you spread light and positivity to those around you. Expand your understanding of spirituality and knowledge. Seek wisdom through books, courses, or by connecting with like-minded individuals. As you continuously learn and grow, you open yourself to new insights and experiences. This makes it clear that the journey within is truly transformative.

By embracing the divine light, we can find solace. We can unlock our true potential and spread light in the world. Remember, the power lies within you. Take the lead and prepare everyone with your words, dispelling the darkness of confusion. Embrace the divine light and allow it to guide you toward peace and strength.

After this incredible experience, when I returned to the practical world, I began my work. Seeing the pictures of Baba scattered with devotion, I felt a pang of sadness and said, "I want only to serve Him. I will truly live for Him and die for Him." This mantra-like expression became radiant and beautiful just for me. After that, it settled in my heart with a serene smile.

It was Truly the Power of Inner Wisdom

Inner wisdom is a powerful tool that guides us in our decision-making process. It is the voice of our soul that speaks to us and provides guidance from a higher power. Though we may not always fully understand the message, trusting our inner wisdom and following its guidance is essential.

In my own experience, I felt a strong inner intuition to focus solely on Baba's work. This intuition was like a mirror reflecting the truth that Baba's presence was within me. By listening to my inner wisdom and dedicating myself to his work, I found a sense of purpose and fulfillment.

I have realized that time is an unstoppable force that continuously moves forward. It waits for no one and stops for no one. With time, prophets and messengers come and go, leaving behind their teachings and memories. These memories shape our lives, influencing our choices and actions. Some memories bring us joy and inspiration, while others serve as lessons and reminders. It is up to us to hold onto goodness in our lives and keep negativity at bay, while also creating a world filled with love, compassion, and understanding.

When we focus on the positive aspects of our lives, we create a ripple effect that spreads positivity and goodness.

By embracing Sai Baba's teachings and dedicating ourselves to his work, we can bring positive change within ourselves and in the world around us. Through our actions and choices, we can make a difference. I have chosen this path for myself, and this is a very important reason behind my decision.

Let us now explore the core principles of Sai Baba that can truly transform our lives.

The Power to Spread the Word of God and Importance of Devotion towards God

There are moments in life when we find ourselves in awe of someone who is capable of spreading the word of God effortlessly. We may wonder how they possess so many thoughts that touch lives and how they have the ability to leave such a profound impact with those thoughts. The truth is, that these individuals are merely vessels through which God's message flows. They do not seek credit for

themselves but understand the importance of surrender at the feet of the Lord.

The power to spread God's word and the significance of surrendering to Him lies in recognizing that they help us accept what we are truly worthy of. Often, we find ourselves chasing after things we desire in life – dreams, ambitions, and goals – and we strive tirelessly to achieve them.

This is a fundamental truth that we must accept. We don't always get what we want. Life has its own way of guiding us toward what we truly deserve. Sometimes, what we are deserving of is far beyond our imagination. Life leads us in that direction, and the true guru (Sadguru) helps guide us along that path.

The Unexpected Nature of God's Blessings

God works in mysterious ways, and His blessings can come to us in ways we least expect. When we surrender ourselves to the divine and let go of our desires and expectations, we receive what is right for us in God's eyes. It is important to remember that God's plans are far greater and more intricate than our own. Each of us has a divine purpose, and trusting in His plan is our duty.

Understanding the Concept of Worthiness

Worthiness is often misunderstood as something that is earned or achieved. However, worthiness is not always tied to our actions or accomplishments. It is a reflection of our faith, devotion, and surrender to the divine. When we surrender to God, we align ourselves with His will, and in return, we become deserving of the blessings He bestows upon us.

The Role of Faith in Surrender

Deep faith is required for surrender at the feet of the Divine. It is a complete trust in their divine wisdom. When we surrender, we dispel our fears, doubts, and insecurities, entrusting our faith into their hands. Through this act of surrender, we allow God to work in our lives, guiding us along the path that has been destined for us. Surrendering to the Lord is not always easy.

For this, we must let go of the need for control and embrace the unknown. When we surrender, we acknowledge that we do not have all the answ ers.

God's plan is greater than our own. It is a humble experience that allows us to grow spiritually and deepen our relationship with the Divine.

The Power to Spread God's Word

As previously mentioned, the power to spread God's word lies in those who can effortlessly share the divine message, they are a medium. They understand that they are not the authors of the message but rather chosen messengers of the Lord. By sharing this message, they are capable of impacting many lives and bringing about positive change in the world.

Their humility and dedication to the will of the Lord allow

them to become instruments of His love and grace.

Dedication, faith, and humility towards the Lord is a powerful act. For this, we must relinquish our own desires and trust in His divine plan. By surrendering to Him, we become worthy instruments to spread His message and positively impact the lives of others. So let us dedicate ourselves at the Lord's feet and allow His love and grace to guide our spiritual journey.

Some Wonderful Thoughts of Sai Baba Related to Life

How Do Changes Come in Life?

In life, we often find ourselves walking a solitary path. As we journey, we encounter various individuals who connect with us. There are events that shape us, and miracles that happen to us. Sometimes, it's the people we connect with, and other times, it's the events that unfold before us.

During those important moments, we realize who our allies are and who our adversaries are! It is always essential to remember that when you have people's trust, never let it diminish. Even when facing difficulties and challenges, never lose faith in God's tests. Instead, use those trials to engage with them, stay connected, and remain in their presence. You will find that they will be your greatest supporters. Look towards them and speak the truth, as that is when they will return to you after some time.

The Importance of Connections

Life is a journey that we begin alone, but the people we meet along the way make it meaningful. Each person we connect with becomes a part of our story, shaping who we are! These connections teach us valuable lessons. They empower and guide us, and sometimes even lead us to unexpected miracles. Therefore, cherish these relationships and never underestimate their power in our lives.

Embracing Life's Events

Life is filled with unexpected events, both good and bad. Sometimes, these events may seem like challenges or failures, but they often present themselves as hidden blessings. They provide us with opportunities to learn, grow, and become stronger and more resilient. Instead of resisting or becoming upset with these events, embracing them allows us to make the most of every situation and even find a glimmer of hope in the darkest moments.

The Power of Miracles

Miracles are extraordinary events that defy logical explanations. They are moments when the impossible becomes possible, restoring hope in adverse circumstances. Miracles can happen at any time and in any place. They remind us of the limitless potential and wonder of life. We should never lose faith in the power of miracles, as they have the ability to transform our lives and fill us with hope and gratitude.

Trust in God's Tests

Life is a series of tests, challenges, and obstacles that we must face. These tests are presented to us by a higher power to help us grow, learn, and become the best versions of ourselves. Trust that these tests are not meant to break us but to build us. Have faith that God knows what we are capable of, and these tests are opportunities for us to prove our strength and resilience.

In summary, as we journey through life, it is crucial to

remember that the people we connect with and the events we encounter shape our path. Miracles happen when we least expect them. God's tests are opportunities for growth and self-discovery. Enjoy the journey, stay connected with your allies, and always remain true to yourself. With faith and resilience, you can navigate through any dangerous or magnificent turns life may present.

In the following paragraphs, we will explore the power of faith through some true stories.

The Power of Faith

Life can sometimes present us with unexpected challenges. We may face difficult situations where traditional solutions fail to work. There is a force greater than any medication or therapy—it's the power of faith and blessings. Today, we will learn about the incredible story of Bhimji Patil, who overcame a serious illness through the strength of his faith.

A Miraculous Journey

Bhimji Patil was afflicted with tuberculosis (TB), a disease once considered incurable. He tried various treatments, but none seemed to help. Feeling helpless, he decided to seek solace in a higher power. Patil surrendered his pain to the divine presence of Baba Sai. With a heart full of devotion, he prayed for healing and blessings.

Baba Sai accepted his prayers with immense grace. At that time, TB was regarded as a deadly disease with no known cure. However, despite all obstacles, Patil's health began to miraculously improve.

The power of Baba Sai's blessings filled his heart, and his faith became the guiding light on his path. The strength of his belief completely healed him.

One More Test of Faith

I experienced a similar event when I was seriously ill. The significance of Sai's miracles was a hit on television. For three days, I suffered from a high fever of 104.4 degrees Fahrenheit, and my condition didn't improve. Drowning in an ocean of despair and tears, I turned to Baba Sai for guidance. I asked, "Baba, my program is airing on TV. No matter how sick I am, I still want to present the show. If I don't get better, it will cause a disruption. The medicine

isn't working; what should I do?" Sai Baba, with his divine wisdom, replied to me. He advised me to take neem leaves, mix them with vibhuti (sacred ash), and heat them. He assured me that consuming this mixture would bring me relief. Trusting his words, I followed his advice and recovered completely.

These stories reveal the immense power of faith and blessings. When faced with seemingly impossible situations, turning to a higher power can lead to incredible transformations. Whether it's through prayers, meditation, or receiving guidance from a spiritual guru, faith has the ability to heal even the most challenging circumstances. When we let go of our worries and trust in divine power, we open ourselves up to receive blessings beyond our understanding. It is this unwavering faith that allows miracles to happen and grants us the strength to overcome any obstacles.

The Power of Blessings

Blessings play a crucial role in our lives. They are a divine expression of love and compassion that showers upon us from a higher power. Just as Bhima Ji Patil experienced miraculous healing through his faith in Sai Baba, blessings have the capacity to transform our lives in unimaginable ways. When we receive blessings, we are infused with positive energy and divine grace. This energy guides and protects us, helping us navigate the challenges of life.

Blessings bring inner peace, strength, and clarity to our minds, allowing us to face any adverse situation with courage and resilience. They empower us to overcome obstacles and foster a sense of hope, enabling us to tackle life's difficulties with grace. In essence, blessings serve as a reminder of the higher powers at work in our lives and encourage us to trust in the journey ahead.

To conclude we can say that, in a world where modern medicine and traditional solutions may sometimes fall short, it is essential to remember the power of faith and blessings. The story of Bhima Ji Patil serves as a powerful reminder that when we open ourselves to the Divine, miracles can happen. By embracing faith and receiving blessings from a higher power, we can find solace, strength, and healing even in the most challenging times. This enduring belief in the transformative power of faith can guide us through life's uncertainties and inspire us to trust in the process.

A Devotee's Transformative Journey

From Collector's Office to Shirdi – Transformation of Life by Divine Touch

A devotional song singer, Dasganu was sent by the Collector's office to Shirdi to seek the blessings of Baba. As soon as he set foot on the sacred land, he felt the divine presence of God in the form of Sai Baba. Overwhelmed with emotions, Dasganu fell at Baba's feet, dedicating his entire life to singing devotional songs in Shirdi. This marked the beginning of an extraordinary journey for the humble singer devotee. But what set this ordinary devotee apart, allowing him to capture the world's attention through his unique perspective?

Let's learn about the intriguing story of the singer who played an important role in Baba's life. Dasganu's devotion and dedication were unwavering. He was an extraordinary individual who played a significant role in shaping Baba's life. The world needs to know and understand how he became the motivating force behind spreading Baba's message to the world!

Unveiling the Mystery

Before we reveal his identity, let's explore how this individual succeeded in capturing Baba's attention and promoting his teachings. Dasganu, whose presence held great significance in Baba's life, had a profound impact on shaping his journey. He had immense faith in Baba's teachings and worked tirelessly to ensure that his message reached far and wide.

His dedication and unwavering belief served as a guiding

light for all those who came to Shirdi in search of spiritual knowledge. Through his relentless efforts, this extraordinary individual made sure that Baba's teachings reached people from all walks of life.

His commitment to spreading love, compassion, and tolerance was truly inspirational. His legacy continues to inspire countless individuals even today. Through his selfless actions and unwavering devotion, he left an indelible mark on the hearts of many.

In a world filled with doubt and skepticism, he was one of those extraordinary individuals who embodied the teachings of a mysterious figure known by the name of Baba. Baba, a revered spiritual leader, preached the importance of selflessness and dedicating oneself to the welfare of society. Dasganu, whose story we have shared today, is a living testament to these values.

The Power of Sai Baba's Throne

Once upon a time, a mother witnessed something extraordinary. She saw Sai Baba seated on a throne, and she could hardly believe her eyes. Baba's eyes were closed, as if he were in deep meditation. However, when Sai Baba opened his eyes, it felt as though he was truly reigning over the world from his royal seat.

Spiritual Impact

The throne of Sai Baba left a profound spiritual impact on those who witnessed it. The mother, mesmerized by the sight of Baba seated on the throne, felt as if he possessed the power to control the universe and guide it with his divine presence.

Sai Baba's throne symbolized his authority and divine power. It represented not just a specific community or group but his role as a spiritual guide and leader for the

entire world. His presence on the throne was a testament to his universal reign and his ability to lead humanity toward enlightenment.

In Sai Baba's teachings, his throne held profound significance. It was not merely a physical object but a symbol of his spiritual authority and his deep connection with the divine. By sitting on the throne, Baba was able to transmit his spiritual energy, reaching out to his disciples and devotees. This throne represented the spiritual journey that Baba's followers had embarked on. It served as a reminder of the ultimate goal of spiritual knowledge and attainment. For those seeking Baba's guidance, the throne stood as a constant source of inspiration and motivation, embodying the path toward enlightenment.

The Significance of Sai Baba's Throne

The significance of Sai Baba's throne was immense for those fortunate enough to witness him seated upon it. It was seen as a divine blessing, as the energy and vibrations emanating from the throne were believed to possess transformative powers, capable of healing and guiding individuals on their spiritual journey. Devotees often sought Baba's blessings during these moments by offering prayers and receiving his guidance, seeing it as an opportunity to connect with the divine and attain spiritual solace and wisdom.

Sai Baba's throne was not just a physical object but symbolized his spiritual authority and his ability to guide humanity towards enlightenment. It was a powerful representation of his divine presence and a beacon for those seeking inner peace and spiritual growth.

This served as a source of inspiration, blessings, and a divine connection for his devotees. Witnessing Baba seated on his throne was an awe-inspiring experience that left an indelible impression on those fortunate enough to witness it. It was not just a moment of spiritual significance but also a deeply personal encounter with the divine, offering a sense of peace, purpose, and connection to all who experienced it.

Lessons for Life

Aushim - Through the story of Sai, we can learn valuable lessons that can be applied to our own lives. His teachings emphasize the importance of selflessness, compassion, and love. He taught his followers to serve others without expecting any reward and to treat all beings with kindness and respect.

Selflessness: Putting the needs of others before our own is a virtue that Sai Baba exemplified. He tirelessly served the poor, the sick, and those in need without expecting anything in return. His life is a reminder of how true fulfillment comes from giving and serving without seeking personal gain.

Compassion: Sai Baba's heart was filled with compassion for all living beings. He showed kindness and empathy to every person who came before him, regardless of their social status or background. His compassion was not limited to a select few but extended to everyone, reflecting his deep care for humanity as a whole.

Love: Love was at the core of Sai Baba's teachings. He believed that love had the power to heal all wounds and bridge all divisions. His unconditional love touched the hearts of many and continues to inspire people even today. Through love, Baba demonstrated how to bring peace and unity into the world, breaking barriers and fostering harmony.

The Importance of the Temple

The construction of the temple in Shirdi stands as a testament to Sai Baba's enduring legacy. It symbolizes the unwavering faith and devotion people have towards him. This temple has become a pilgrimage site for millions of devotees who come seeking solace, blessings, and guidance.

The temple's creation is a reflection of the lasting impact of Sai Baba's life and message. As we delve into the chapters of his story, we open our hearts and minds to the wisdom and love that emanates from his words.

The Power of Selflessness

Selflessness is a virtue that has been celebrated throughout history. It is the act of putting the needs and desires of others before one's own. In a world where personal gain often seems to dominate, selflessness has become a rare quality. However, the importance of selflessness cannot be understated. It is not only a moral imperative but also has the power to transform individuals and society as a whole.

Selflessness in Everyday Life

Selflessness isn't limited to grand gestures or heroic acts. It can be practiced in our daily lives through small, meaningful actions. Consider a mother who prioritizes her child's needs over her own, sacrificing her comfort for the well-being of her child. Or a volunteer who spends their free time helping the less fortunate without expecting anything in return. These acts of selflessness may seem insignificant, but they have the power to create a ripple effect. Such actions inspire others to act selflessly as well, fostering a more compassionate and empathetic society. Selflessness encourages a culture where kindness and understanding flourish, making a significant difference in the lives of others and in our communities.

The Rewards of Selflessness

Selflessness is beneficial not only for society but also for the individuals who practice it. When we prioritize the needs of others, we experience a sense of satisfaction and purpose. Research has shown that selflessness can improve our mental and physical well-being. It reduces stress and enhances our emotional resilience, even boosting our immune system. Moreover, selflessness has the power to transform our relationships. When we act with genuine kindness, we build trust, strengthen bonds, and foster a sense of unity with others. These connections enrich our lives and create a supportive community, highlighting the profound impact that selfless actions can have on both ourselves and those around us.

Overcoming Selfishness

Overcoming selfishness and embracing selflessness is no easy task. It requires a fundamental shift in our mindset and a conscious effort to prioritize the needs of others. One effective way to cultivate selflessness is by practicing empathy. Empathy allows us to understand and share the feelings of others, enabling us to act with compassion and selflessness. Another important aspect of selflessness is gratitude. When we appreciate what we have and acknowledge the blessings in our lives, we become more inclined to extend a helping hand to others. Gratitude fosters a sense of abundance, making it easier for us to be generous and supportive, ultimately creating a more compassionate and connected community. By nurturing these qualities, we can gradually reduce selfish tendencies and cultivate a more selfless approach to life.

The Call for Selflessness

The call for selflessness is not limited to a select few individuals. It is a call that resonates with everyone, regardless of their background or circumstances. Selflessness is not merely about grand gestures or sacrificing one's happiness; it is about finding small ways to make a difference in the lives of others. The next time you have the opportunity to act selflessly, remember the story of Krishna and Draupadi. Their tale, shared later in this book, serves as a powerful reminder of the impact of selfless actions. Keep in mind the transformative power of selflessness as you strive to bring about positive change in your own life and in the world around you.

The Power of Dignity and Service

Have you ever contemplated the importance of self-respect and serving others? We will now shed light on the profound message conveyed by Baba, often regarded as a miraculous figure. Baba's teachings encourage us to enhance our self-esteem and embrace our capabilities, ultimately guiding us toward true humanity and spiritual fulfillment.

The Journey of Self-Respect

Self-respect is the foundation of a fulfilling life. It is an empowering force that enables individuals to reach new heights and overcome obstacles. Baba's profound words emphasize the importance of enhancing our self-esteem. He states, "The day you elevate your self-respect, the day you honor yourself and acknowledge your capabilities, is the day you become a strong advocate for true humanity and spiritual values." This message reminds us that self-respect is not selfish; it involves recognizing our worth and embracing our unique abilities. Baba also emphasizes the importance of service alongside self-respect. By engaging in selfless acts of kindness, we affirm our true capabilities as human beings.

Service allows us to contribute to the welfare of society and uplift others. Baba's message encourages us to reflect on our actions and consider what contributions we can make in this world. By serving others, we not only create a positive impact but also experience personal growth and fulfillment.

Baba is often regarded as a miraculous figure. People believe that connecting with Baba can bring miraculous experiences into their lives. However, it is important to recognize that Baba's teachings extend beyond personal gain. His message focuses on self-respect, true service, and spiritual values. Baba reminds us that the mentality of expecting miracles is driven by selfishness. Instead, we should strive to be selfless and offer our support and love to others without any hidden agenda. Embracing this philosophy can lead to genuine connections and a more compassionate world.

A Journey Towards Selfless Service

Baba's message challenges us to examine our intentions and purposes. Are we motivated by personal gain and recognition, or are we genuinely committed to serving others? This self-reflection allows us to embark on a transformative journey towards selflessness. By separating ourselves from selfish desires, we can truly make a positive impact in the world and foster a sense of unity and compassion within our communities. Each act of selfless service not only enriches the lives of those we help but also elevates our own spirit, creating a ripple effect of goodwill and kindness.

Conclusion: The power of self-respect and service should not be underestimated. Baba's message reminds us that by enhancing our self-respect and engaging in selfless acts of service, we can become catalysts for positive change. Let us embrace the wisdom given by Baba and strive to live a life that prioritizes true humanity and spiritual fulfillment. Together, we can build a world that thrives on compassion, understanding, and selfless service.

Divine Influence of Sai Baba

Sai Baba's teachings have had a profound impact on the lives of millions. His wisdom transcends religious boundaries and resonates with people from all walks of life. Through his teachings, Sai Baba emphasizes the importance of love, compassion, and righteousness in our daily lives.

The Search for Inner Peace

Sai Baba's teachings emphasize the importance of finding inner peace amidst the turmoil of daily life. In today's fast-paced world, it's easy to lose connection with our inner selves amidst the constant hustle and bustle. However, by following the principles laid down by Sai Baba, we can learn to develop a peaceful and calm mindset, regardless of the circumstances around us.

Living with Purpose

One of Sai Baba's core teachings is the importance of living a purposeful life. He encourages us to discover our true desires and work towards fulfilling them. By aligning our actions with our purpose, we can lead a more meaningful and fulfilling life.

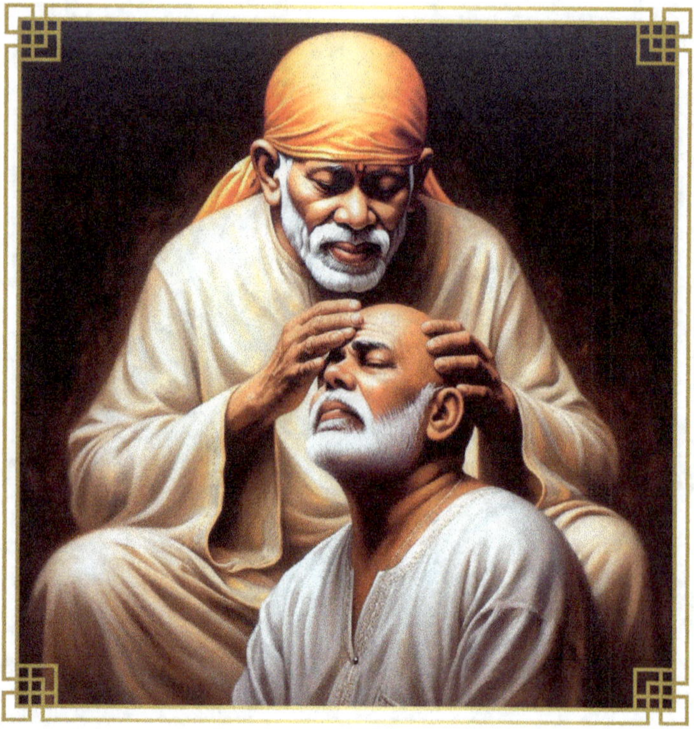

The Transformative Power of Faith

Sai Baba's teachings highlight the transformative power of faith. He stresses the importance of having unwavering faith in a higher power and trusting in the divine plan. Through faith, we can overcome obstacles and find comfort in times of adversity. In doing so, we experience a profound sense of peace.

Practicing Selfless Service

Sai Baba teaches the value of selfless service and encourages helping those in need. By serving others without any expectation of reward, we not only contribute to the betterment of society but also experience deep fulfillment and inner happiness.

The Path of Devotion

Aushim - In Sai Baba's teachings, devotion plays a significant role. He emphasizes the importance of surrendering to a higher power and cultivating deep feelings of devotion. Through devotion, we can establish a strong connection with the Divine and experience profound spiritual transformation.

Stories of Characters Reaching Great Heights Through the Path of Faith, Trust, and Devotion

From Motorcycle Mechanic to a Spiritual Journey (First Story)

Ravi Talwar, a motorcycle mechanic, found himself at a crossroads in life. As a part-time trainer, he struggled to

find enough work to support himself. With little interest in pursuing further education, Ravi decided to become a motorcycle mechanic, eventually leading him to open his own shop.

This practical choice seemed to define his future, but little did he know that this was just the beginning of a deeper, spiritual journey that would change the course of his life in unexpected ways.

Near Rohtak, Ravi's motorcycle repair shop quickly gained popularity due to his unique approach to customer service. His shop was always bustling with eager customers, not just because of his mechanical skills but because of how he treated his clients. Ravi went beyond the usual mechanic-customer relationship, taking time to establish personal connections with each client. He would engage in informal chats, offer refreshments, and even share anecdotes. People were drawn to his friendly nature and how he made them feel valued.

Despite his success as a mechanic, Ravi had a pragmatic outlook on life. He didn't believe in any higher power or spiritual concepts. His perspective was entirely practical, grounded in the physical world. However, something unexpected was about to happen that would completely alter his beliefs.

One day, a mysterious stranger walked into Ravi's shop. This person exuded an aura of peace and spirituality. They began conversing with Ravi, discussing topics beyond the

scope of motorcycles. Initially, Ravi was skeptical, but as the conversation progressed, he couldn't help but feel intrigued.

Over time, Ravi's interactions with the stranger began to have a profound impact on his life. He started questioning his long-held beliefs and began exploring spirituality in ways he never had before. The stranger introduced Ravi to the idea of surrendering to a higher power, something Ravi had firmly rejected until then. Slowly but surely, Ravi's worldview began to shift.

Gradually, Ravi's shop transformed from a simple motorcycle repair center into a spiritual haven. He began displaying religious symbols and artifacts, dedicating each object to various deities and divine entities. The shop became much more than just a place for mechanical repairs. It evolved into a sanctuary for those seeking solace and guidance.

Ravi's journey from being a motorcycle mechanic to a spiritual guide is a testament to the unpredictability of life. Sometimes, the most unexpected events can lead us down paths we never imagined. Ravi's story is a reminder to keep an open mind and embrace new experiences, as they can bring profound transformations to our lives.

Introduction to Inner Strength (Second Story)

In a small village lived a man named Mohit Rana, known for his arrogance and lack of belief in any higher power. Mohit neither believed in God nor respected any spiritual figures. However, one event changed his perspective forever.

One day, Mohit decided to show off his strength in front of the entire village. He called for a tractor. As the tractor started moving, Mohit felt a surge of energy within himself. He believed that his strength had grown so much that he

could stop the tractor. Filled with this newfound confidence, Mohit stood in front of the approaching tractor.

Unfortunately, the tractor did not stop.

Mohit was run over by the tractor, leaving him severely injured. In that very moment, lying on the ground, he experienced a profound realization. The incident reminded him of the existence of a higher power, a supreme force.

Mohit understood that the strength he once boasted about was nothing compared to the divine power. He realized that his arrogance had blinded him to the truth. From that day onward, Mohit never forgot the incident that shattered his ego and made him recognize his insignificance in front of the universal power.

This event taught Mohit a valuable lesson—to be humble and respectful toward the Supreme Being. He understood that no matter how much strength a person possesses, it pales in comparison to the omnipotent force. Mohit's journey from disbelief to awakening serves as a reminder to all of us that we must never let our ego blind us. It is important to acknowledge and respect divine power. No matter how strong or successful we become, there will always be a greater force above us.

Let us learn from Mohit's experience and cultivate humility in our hearts.

The Power to Empower Girls (Third Story)

One auspicious day, Suresh was casually reading the newspaper. As he opened it, he saw a small picture of Baba. He closed his eyes and silently prayed, "Om Sai Ram." Within moments, an overwhelming wave of emotions surged within him. These emotions grew so intense that even the picture of Baba seemed to speak to him, saying, "Son, you may not have called me, but I know you are my true son. In this village, where many girls are suffering, the

time for change has come. If you do not do it, no one will."

Everyone has an objection to not educating these girls and not providing them with opportunities. "Let's embark on the journey of empowerment." Hearing this, Suresh started a mission to empower girls in his village with a renewed determination. He believed that education was the key to their liberation and he was ready to take the first step. Three years later, Suresh successfully changed the lives of 70 girls in the same village.

Education is a powerful tool that can break the cycle of poverty and discrimination. By not providing girls access to education, Suresh was denying them the opportunity to create a better future for themselves. Education empowers girls to dream big, pursue their passions, and become independent individuals.

During his journey to empower girls, Suresh faced many challenges. The deeply entrenched patriarchal mindset in the village was resistant to change. Many families believed that a girl's place was at home, not in the classroom. Suresh had to explain to all the parents the importance of education and the long-term benefits it would bring to their daughters.

Suresh realized that merely providing education was not enough. He established a safe space for girls where they could learn and grow. He encouraged community involvement and organized workshops to educate parents about the value of their daughters' education.

One by one, Suresh broke down the barriers that stood in the way of girls' education. He challenged social norms and fought against gender discrimination. He fought for his community. Through his unwavering determination and support from his community, Suresh paved the way for a new generation of educated and empowered girls.

Suresh's efforts went beyond the boundaries of his village. The success stories of empowered girls inspired others to follow in their footsteps. The village became a model for gender equality and education, serving as an exemplary case for other communities to emulate.

Suresh's journey is far from over. He continues to work tirelessly to empower girls and create a more just society. His dream is that every girl, both in his village and beyond, receives quality education and the opportunity to realize her full potential. Suresh's legacy will live on through the lives he has transformed and the generations of empowered girls to come.

The Story of Krishna and Draupadi

The story of Krishna and Draupadi in the epic "Mahabharata" exemplifies the essence of selflessness. Draupadi, facing immense humiliation in the royal court, called out for divine help. Seeing her in distress, the divine avatar Krishna selflessly intervened. He provided Draupadi with an endless supply of garments, protecting her dignity and shielding her from disgrace.

Krishna's act of selflessness not only preserved Draupadi's honor but also made him a symbol of hope and justice. His actions remind us of the power of selfless service and standing up for what is right in times of crisis.

The Story of Draupadi

It is an ancient tale that resonates with the concept of selflessness. Draupadi, a powerful and influential woman in Indian mythology, was gifted with a unique ability— the power to manifest desires. However, unlike many who might use such a gift for personal gain, Draupadi chose to use her strength to help others.

Unlike many individuals today who seek material wealth or fame, Draupadi's desires were focused on making a difference in the lives of others. Her mission was to uplift those who were marginalized, disabled, or orphaned. Her story teaches us the value of selfless service and the importance of using one's abilities for the greater good rather than for personal advancement.

Empowering Individuals: The Desire to Help Others (Selflessness)

In today's world, it's common to prioritize personal interests over the needs of others. Often, we see a lack of empathy with a focus on individual gain. However, there are still individuals who genuinely desire to help those around them, without caring for personal benefit. This selflessness is truly remarkable, as it demonstrates the power to bring positive change in society.

Draupadi's desire to help those on the margins stemmed from her understanding of their struggles. She recognized the importance of empowering these individuals so they could overcome social barriers. By advocating for their rights and welfare, Draupadi sought to create a more inclusive and just society.

Draupadi was deeply committed to supporting people with disabilities. She believed that their physical limitations should not define their worth or abilities. She worked tirelessly to ensure that they received the support and opportunities they deserved.

Orphaned children held a special place in Draupadi's heart. She understood the challenges they faced without the guidance and love of their parents. Draupadi's desire to help these children was driven by her belief that every child deserves a nurturing and caring environment. Draupadi's story reminds us of the importance of selflessness in our lives. Often, we become consumed by our own desires and overlook the needs of those around us. However, by adopting a selfless mindset, we can create a wave of positivity and have a lasting impact on society.

In a world where selfishness is often prioritized, Draupadi's story stands as an inspiration. Her selflessness and desire to help others without expecting personal gain are testaments to the power of compassion and empathy. Let us strive to follow in her footsteps and bring about change in the lives of others, for it is through selfless actions that we can truly transform society.

Discovering Your Potential

The day you enhance your self-respect and realize your true potential, you will experience a new energy that will lead you to achieve great accomplishments in life. This message, shared by Baba, encourages individuals not only to serve themselves but also to contribute to the welfare of society. With a sense of selflessness, this can be done effortlessly.

Baba's Miracles

Many people consider Baba to be a miraculous figure. They believe that when they connect with him, miracles happen. It's important to note that there is also a level of self-interest involved in this belief. Baba truly possesses extraordinary qualities. His teachings go beyond personal gain.

The Power of Service

Baba emphasizes the importance of serving others. By serving others, we not only create a positive impact on their lives but also experience personal growth and satisfaction. The act of selflessly helping others allows us to hone our abilities and discover what we are truly capable of achieving.

Self-empowerment and self-actualization are significant aspects of Baba's teachings. He encourages individuals to build their self-esteem and have faith in their abilities. When we recognize our skills and potential, we can overcome obstacles and pursue our passions. In this way, we can bring about change in the world. Every individual has the power to create positive transformation within themselves.

Embracing Challenges

One of the key messages imparted by Baba is the importance of accepting challenges. Instead of shying away from difficulties, we should view them as opportunities for growth. By stepping out of our comfort zones and confronting adverse situations with determination, we can develop resilience and gain valuable life lessons. Embracing challenges not only strengthens our character but also empowers us to navigate through life's obstacles with confidence.

Transforming Lives

Baba's teachings hold the power to transform lives. Through his guidance, individuals can uncover their true potential and find meaning and purpose in their existence. The journey of self-empowerment and service is not always easy, but it is a meaningful path to take.

In the end, Baba's message encourages individuals to enhance their self-esteem and channel their energy into discovering what they can achieve in life. Serving others and contributing to the welfare of society is a central aspect of his teachings. Embracing this mindset can lead to profound personal growth and a positive impact on the world around us.

Some people may see Baba as a miraculous figure driven by self-interest, but his true essence lies in inspiring individuals to recognize their potential and make a positive impact on the world. Embracing challenges, adopting self-empowerment, and welcoming transformation are all integral parts of this journey. Take the first step today towards self-discovery and embark on the path of personal development and service to others.

The Importance of Krishna's Words for Leading a Beautiful Life

The words of Krishna carry immense weight and knowledge. His message transcends a conversation in the Mahabharata and remains relevant in our lives today. The principles of selflessness and sacrifice can be applied to various aspects of life, whether they pertain to personal relationships, professional endeavors, or social contributions. By embracing Krishna's teachings, we can strive to create a more compassionate and harmonious world.

Changing Perspectives

It is human nature to be caught up in personal circumstances and concerns. However, Arjuna's advice from Krishna serves as a reminder to shift our perspectives. By redirecting our thoughts and actions toward the welfare of others, we not only change ourselves but also impact those around us. True transformation can only occur through selflessness and sacrifice.

The Importance of Sacrifice

Krishna's words also illuminate the significance of sacrifice. He urged Arjuna to stop focusing on personal losses and instead concentrate on the larger picture. Sacrifices in life are inevitable, and through these sacrifices, one can truly contribute to the welfare of humanity. Rather than fixating on his own troubles, Krishna encouraged Arjuna to see the bigger picture and consider the consequences of his actions on the Kauravas.

Amidst the grand narrative of the Mahabharata, Krishna's conversation with Arjuna serves as a reminder of the importance of selflessness and sacrifice. By relinquishing personal desires and focusing on the welfare of others, we can bring about positive change.

Krishna's teachings are not confined to the context of the narratives; they possess universal significance. Known as a divine incarnation, Krishna's words have had a profound impact throughout history. From his initial teachings to his various later incarnations, Krishna's words continue to hold relevance today. We will explore the essence of Krishna's ultimate message.

The Fear of Death

A central theme in Krishna's teachings is the fear of death. He emphasizes that one should not fear death, as it is merely a transition from one realm to another. By overcoming the fear of death, individuals can fully embrace life and live without any apprehension.

The Souls of Children

Children, due to their purity and innocence, have a remarkable receptivity to Krishna's teachings. They are free from social constraints and are more receptive to truth. Their ability to understand and embrace these teachings often surpasses that of many adults.

Overcoming Depression

Depression is a prevalent issue in today's society. Krishna's words offer solace and hope to those suffering from it. By understanding the ephemeral nature of life, individuals can find strength in knowing that difficult times will pass, and happiness will eventually return.

The Power of Time

Time is a universal force that affects everyone. Krishna's message teaches individuals about the significance of recognizing the power of time and using it wisely. By appreciating the value of each moment, individuals can make the most of their time on Earth.

Journey Towards Self-Realization

Krishna's teachings guide individuals on the path to self-realization. Through self-reflection and introspection, one can unveil their true self and purpose. This journey towards self-awareness is transformative, leading to a deeper understanding of oneself and the world. Krishna's words resonate through the ages, continuously inspiring individuals to live a meaningful life. His teachings provide guidance on overcoming fear, finding inner peace, and embracing the journey of self-discovery. By applying the wisdom in Krishna's words, individuals can navigate the complexities of life and experience true fulfillment.

What is Happiness & Satisfaction?

We will delve deeply into the concept of happiness and its significance. Happiness is a personal state that everyone strives to achieve. It is often associated with feelings of satisfaction and fulfillment.

Perspective of Bulleh Shah

Baba Bulleh Shah, who was a poet and a mystic, was once asked by Babul Shastri about the secret to attaining happiness. In response, Bulleh Shah mentioned that he had never seen his own hand, implying that happiness cannot be found through physical possessions. He believed that happiness exists beyond the material world.

There was a question posed to Sai Baba regarding what his disciple Lakshmi had said. Lakshmi remarked that Baba could only survive by eating once a day, to which Baba replied, "When it comes to food, who wins? I have won because I can live without it."

Both Bulleh Shah and Sai Baba emphasize that true happiness does not lie in material wealth or physical comforts. Their argument is that the pursuit of mere riches or food does not lead to lasting satisfaction.

Finding Happiness in Simplicity

The teachings of Bulleh Shah and Sai Baba highlight the importance of simplicity in attaining happiness. They advocate for a life where an individual is not bound by the desire for material wealth or excessive indulgence. By embracing simplicity, one can free themselves from the endless pursuit of possessions and find satisfaction in the present moment.

Spreading Happiness to Others

Both Bulleh Shah and Sai Baba believed in the power of spreading happiness to others. They encouraged individuals to focus on helping others and bringing joy to those around them. By extending kindness, love, and compassion, a person can create a ripple effect of happiness in the world. The pursuit of happiness is an intrinsic part of the human experience. Bulleh Shah and Sai Baba remind us that true happiness cannot be found in external possessions

or material activities. It resides within us and is nurtured through simplicity, compassion, and selflessness. By understanding the essence of happiness, we can lead more fulfilling lives and contribute to the happiness of others.

Have you ever taken a moment to sit in solitude and reflect on your achievements and experiences? Contemplating the various aspects of our lives can be a valuable practice for self-discovery and self-awareness. We will explore the concepts of satisfaction and happiness, examining how they relate to the different facets of our lives.

Finding Satisfaction in Different Aspects of Life

As we journey through life, we often find ourselves pursuing various goals and aspirations. These can include personal achievements such as education, starting a business, getting married, or even dedicating ourselves to serving our parents. The source of our greatest happiness can vary for each individual. One question that frequently arises is about the concepts of satisfaction and how we attain it in our lives.

Education and Knowledge

For many individuals, the pursuit of education and the acquisition of knowledge bring immense happiness and satisfaction. Learning about various subjects, exploring new ideas, and expanding one's intellectual horizons can foster a sense of achievement and fulfillment.

Career and Business

Another area where people often seek satisfaction is in their professional lives. Building a successful career or starting a business can evoke a strong sense of achievement and fulfillment. Witnessing the fruits of one's hard work and seeing the growth and success of one's efforts can be incredibly gratifying.

Serving Parents

One aspect of finding satisfaction and happiness that is often overlooked is serving one's parents. The bond between parents and children is unique and special. Caring for one's parents, respecting them, and being present for them can evoke profound feelings of satisfaction and fulfillment.

The True Nature of Happiness

While the aforementioned areas can bring satisfaction and happiness, it is essential to recognize that true happiness lies within us. External achievements and relationships can certainly contribute to our well-being, but lasting happiness comes from within. Human satisfaction and happiness are rooted in self-acceptance, self-love, and personal growth. This occurs when we accept ourselves, acknowledge our strengths and weaknesses, and work towards personal development. Only then can we experience genuine happiness.

Conclusion:

As we go through different stages of life, we must pause and reflect on what truly brings us satisfaction. While external achievements and relationships can contribute to our happiness, ultimately, our relationship with ourselves determines our overall well-being. Striving for personal growth, self-acceptance, and self-love will pave the way for authentic and lasting happiness. So, take some time to reflect and ask yourself, "Where do I find the most happiness and satisfaction?"

The answer will be unique for each person and can ultimately lead you on a path of self-discovery and fulfillment.

Other Literature Related to Sai Baba

In the realm of literature, many scholars have presented the story of Sai Baba in various forms. Numerous noteworthy books by devotees of Sai Baba discuss the impact of Sai devotion and spiritual dialogues on people's lives.

Sai Baba's monumental text, "Shri Sai Baba Satcharitra", describes Baba's countless miracles. These are the stories that took place during Sai Baba's lifetime, through which surrendered devotees experienced the direct benefits of Sai Baba's presence.

When a devotee reads these stories today, they may not

immediately believe in those events; however, they are indeed the absolute truth. The true guru represents God. He can accomplish what he desires through divine will.

Nigobind Raghunath Dabholkar was a renowned scholar of Sanskrit and Marathi. After retiring from his job, he sought out Sai Baba for a purpose. Sai Baba had faith in Dabholkar's wisdom and placed his divine hand on his head, emphasizing the importance of writing scriptures.

The journey of a saint is different from the moment of their birth. They are the bearers of divine knowledge, and their purpose is to guide humanity toward a higher spiritual path. Through their actions and teachings, they strive to bring transformation to the lives of those fortunate enough to encounter them.

The story of Sai has profoundly impacted countless individuals' lives. It serves as proof of the power of faith and devotion. The pages of his life, written by Himanshu Pandya, have become a source of inspiration for millions. Reading about his miracles and teachings ignites a spark of faith in the hearts of people.

A significant aspect of Sai Baba's story is the unwavering faith and devotion of his followers. The miracles he described are not merely fictional tales; they are real-life experiences of those who have witnessed his divine intervention in their lives. These miracles serve as reminders that a higher power is guiding our paths. An important book in this regard is "Sai Satcharitra".

The Beginning of Sai Satcharitra

When Hemad Pant began writing "Sai Satcharitra", he had no idea that this book would become such an important spiritual scripture, connecting people to the holy temple of Shirdi. He did not realize that the words he wrote would lead to the construction of a magnificent temple in Shirdi, which would become a place of immense faith for millions of devotees. This is the power and influence of a saint born on this earth. Such individuals possess the ability to convey a message that transcends worldly desires and objectives.

"Sai Satcharitra"

The source of faith, "Sai Satcharitra", is a sacred book that narrates the life and teachings of the revered saint Sai Baba, who resided in Shirdi. This divine text has touched the hearts of countless individuals, strengthened their faith, and guided them in their spiritual journeys. Within the pages of "Sai Satcharitra", readers are transported back to the time when Sai Baba graced the earth, displaying unconditional love and compassion for all.

Through His actions and interactions with devotees, Sai Baba imparted profound knowledge and taught valuable lessons on living a better life. His teachings revolve around the principles of love, truth, and selflessness. He emphasized the necessity of inner transformation and encouraged His followers to lead a righteous and virtuous life.

One of Sai Baba's core teachings is the importance of surrendering to a higher power. He believed that by renouncing ego and desires, individuals could attain spiritual knowledge and experience true bliss. Sai Baba also stressed the significance of serving humanity. He taught that selfless service is a means to connect with the divine and attain completeness. Through acts of compassion and kindness, Sai Baba inspired others to make a positive impact on society.

Additionally, Sai Baba advocated for the unity of all religions. He taught that all paths lead to the same destination and emphasized the need for respect and tolerance towards different beliefs.

Impact on Shirdi

Since the establishment of the Sai Baba temple, Shirdi has become a center for spiritual pilgrimage. People from all walks of life, representing various religions and cultures, come to this sacred place to seek blessings and guidance. The "Sai Satcharitra" plays a significant role in the lives of devotees.

This text serves as a source of inspiration, comfort, and guidance. Through the stories and teachings contained within its pages, readers are reminded of Sai Baba's divine presence and the timeless messages of love and compassion he embodied. Moreover, the "Sai Satcharitra" has transcended geographical boundaries, reaching devotees worldwide. Translations of the book into various languages have enabled people from different countries to connect with Sai Baba's teachings and wisdom.

Journey of Faith

Embarking on a journey with Sai Baba through the "Sai Satcharitra" is a rich and transformative experience. As readers immerse themselves in the narratives and teachings, they gain valuable insights for their spiritual paths. Sai Baba's teachings resonate with individuals of all ages, whether one is facing challenges in life, seeking guidance, or simply in search of solace. The "Sai Satcharitra" serves as a source of hope and strength. Through this sacred text, we explore the life of Sai Baba. Let us embrace the timeless wisdom and teachings that have the power to uplift and transform our lives.

Conclusion:

As captured in the writings of Hemad Pant and other authors, the story of Sai Baba possesses the power to touch hearts and transform lives. It is a narrative of faith, devotion, miracles, and profound teachings.

Spiritual and Natural Healing for Illnesses

The Power of Simple Remedies

Have you ever wondered how some people recover from illnesses so quickly? The answer lies in simple or spiritual remedies that can profoundly impact our health. In this chapter, we will explore the concept of common illnesses and the treatments that can assist in our healing process.

There was a time when Baba performed miraculous cures that left people astonished. He would write about "Bapu Booti", a herbal medicine that has the power to heal even the most painful diseases. One such example is the case of Shold Singh, who suffered from a throat ailment. He was advised to drink a mixture of milk with nuts and beauty herbs, and miraculously, he completely recovered. Now, let's delve deeper into the onset of illnesses and explore how we can find their solutions.

Nature of Common Illnesses

When it comes to common illnesses, we often underestimate their impact. They tend to get lost in the noise of complex diseases, but the truth is that common ailments often suffer from neglect and are viewed as minor inconveniences. However, they hold the key to a happy and healthy life.

Unveiling the Secrets of a Healthy Body

The two pillars of a simple, illness-free life are devotion and peace. At night, when we engage in contemplation, Baba comes to our minds and provides us with all the solutions we need. These solutions can be found in the books we read or the talks we listen to. They serve as gifts in our rooms. When we read or listen to them, we become better and more harmonious individuals.

Use of Natural Materials for Health and Wellness

In today's fast-paced world, finding effective solutions for various health issues can be challenging. However, many people are turning to natural remedies and materials such as balms, sandalwood, and water for their ailments. We will explore the benefits of using these natural substances and learn how they can promote overall well-being.

The Healing Touch of Sandalwood

Sandalwood is another natural ingredient that has been used for centuries due to its numerous health benefits. Its soothing and calming properties make it an effective remedy for stress and anxiety. Applying a paste or oil of sandalwood can also provide relief from skin-related issues such as rashes and irritation. The divine love and touch associated with sandalwood, combined with its use in sacred rituals, enhance its healing properties even further.

Divine Combination: Udi and Water

It is believed that the combined use of udi (sacred ash) and water has powerful healing effects. Udi can be ingested or applied topically in conjunction with water to address various health issues. This divine combination is said to enhance love, faith, and blessings, creating a holistic perspective towards well-being.

Conclusion:

While ordinary ailments may seem insignificant, they can have a significant impact on our lives. By understanding and adopting simple remedies, we can manage these ailments and enjoy a healthy and happy life. Therefore, we should not underestimate the power of simplicity when it comes to our well-being.

By utilizing the power of natural substances like sandalwood, udi, and water, individuals can find effective treatments for their health concerns. These substances, combined with divine love and blessings, can enhance overall well-being and provide relief from various ailments. Embracing the age-old knowledge of natural remedies can be a transformative journey towards a healthier and more balanced life.

Here are some special mantras and songs sung in reverence of Sai Baba:

Hanuman Chalisa

Mujhe Sai Baba Shirdi Bula Lo

Om Chant 108 TImes

Om Shree Sai Nathay Namah

Sai Chalisa

Sai Ram O Mere Sai Ram

About the Book

The book "Sai Vani" sheds light on the profound teachings of Sai Baba and how they can impact our lives. It emphasizes the importance of cultivating a peaceful character that has the power to touch our souls. As you read through the pages of this book, you will undoubtedly create memorable moments with your loved ones and witness long-cherished tasks coming to fruition.

As we delve into the stories of "Sai Vani", we are reminded of the powers of peace, love, and faith. His teachings provide a roadmap for dealing with life's challenges and seeking comfort in times of uncertainty. By incorporating these teachings into our daily lives, we can experience profound transformation and lead a more purposeful and fulfilling existence.